EMPOWERED

2022

VERSES TO INSPIRE

Edited By Daisy Job

First published in Great Britain in 2022 by:

YoungWriters® Est. 1991

Young Writers
Remus House
Coltsfoot Drive
Peterborough
PE2 9BF
Telephone: 01733 890066
Website: www.youngwriters.co.uk

Printed and bound in the UK by BookPrintingUK
Website: www.bookprintinguk.com
YB0520H

⭐ FOREWORD ⭐

Since 1991, here at Young Writers we have celebrated the awesome power of creative writing, especially in young adults where it can serve as a vital method of expressing their emotions and views about the world around them. In every poem we see the effort and thought that each student published in this book has put into their work and by creating this anthology we hope to encourage them further with the ultimate goal of sparking a life-long love of writing.

Our latest competition for secondary school students, Empowered, challenged young writers to consider what was important to them. We wanted to give them a voice, the chance to express themselves freely and honestly, something which is so important for these young adults to feel confident and listened to. They could give an opinion, share a memory, consider a dilemma, impart advice or simply write about something they love. There were no restrictions on style or subject so you will find an anthology brimming with a variety of poetic styles and topics. We hope you find it as absorbing as we have.

We encourage young writers to express themselves and address subjects that matter to them, which sometimes means writing about sensitive or contentious topics. If you have been affected by any issues raised in this book, details on where to find help can be found at www.youngwriters.co.uk/info/other/contact-lines

★ CONTENTS ★

Connie Burling (11) 82

Tom Robinson (11) 83

Edward Penfound (12) 84

Martha Houlder (12) 85

Audrey Hurles (11) 86

Zerrin Dhillon (14) 87

Lee Fuller (14) 88

Evie Drew (12) 89

Isabel Arnott (12) 90

Honey-Rose Howard (13) 91

Emilia Clough (12) 92

Walter Donnelly (12) 93

Ellis Beech (12) 94

Imogen Swygart (13) 95

Chloe Choi (11) 96

Heather Cheryl-Rose 97
Hutchison (12)

Xavier Brame (12) 98

Ruby Chantelle Corner (12) 99

Thea Brunton (12) 100

Molly Clarke Stow (12) 101

Rory Langdon (12) 102

River Churchman (14) 103

Dominic Ng'ang'a (12) 104

Mateo Rodriguez Pariente (12) 105

Freya Brown (13) 106

Edward N Fernandes (12) 107

Olive Brown (12) 108

Clarkson Mantlo (12) 109

Beau O'Gorman (12) 110

Lucy Bridgeman (12) 111

Florence Stannard (12) 112

Eva Murphy (12) 113

Lily Benton (13) 114

Tristan Herridge (12) 115

Tom Hughes (12) 116

Nataylia Jayne Adams (12) 117

Jaiman Bhagat (12) 118

Daniel Etches (12) 119

Bella Thomas (12) 120

Kleins Tocilla (12) 121

Alfie Reynolds (11) 122

Maya Jaiyeola (13) 123

Teddy Joy-Staines (12) 124

Higham Lane School Business And Enterprise College, Nuneaton

Jessica Doughty (14) 125

Hornchurch High School, Hornchurch

Denis Clineanu (13) 126

Kahiron Woodruffe (13) 128

Divine Apinoko (12) 129

Neve Power (11) 130

Alfie Thorne (13) 131

Kian Davies (13) 132

April Brett (11) 133

Max Burgess (12) 134

Ivan Matidonschi (12) 135

Freddie Fisher (12) 136

Taha Mohammed (13) 137

Tegan Harper (12) 138

Max Cole-Theinmaung (12) 139

Sarah Mata (12) 140

Rhsharn Warren (12) 141

Kyara Alves (12) 142

Oliver Kersey (12) 143

Fallon Boxall (12) 144

Mario Oanta (12) 145

Huish Episcopi Academy, Langport

George Khan-Davis (13) 146

Zoë Huntley (13) 147

Elsie Yates (13) 148

Riley Pope (12) 149

Amelia Manning (12) 150

Eleanor Millichip (12) 151

Emily Roberts (13) 152

Hannah Berryman (12) 153

Manchester Settlement, Openshaw

Ravens Wood School, Bromley

Rendcomb College, Rendcomb

Savio Salesian College, Bootle

THE POEMS

Making A Change

What do you think about pollution?
Do you think we need a solution?
All this plastic,
Don't you think it's getting a bit drastic?
Let's all try to save the planet!

We could all plant some trees,
To help save animals like the bees,
You should go buy some seeds,
To help save the planet's needs,
Let's all try to save the planet!

Plastic is killing the planet,
So maybe we could ban it,
We are killing the planet with litter,
Don't you think that's a bit bitter?
Let's all try to save the planet!

Oliver Hayward (12)
Bennett Memorial Diocesan School, Culverden Down

Shining Star

It feels as if all of them are shining like bright stars
Achieving the unachievable
But me, a small speck of dust
No one knows
No one cares about
I feel like a mouse
Trapped in a cage full of cats
Ready to pounce
To tear away at me

When they look upon my work
They sigh
They don't see me trying to work industriously
They look for the good grade
Not to how they can improve
But who will succeed?
And the one who will never exceed
It feels everyone is succeeding
Except me
An outcast
The one who has the label of slothful
They think
Things that hurt
They just don't know

No matter what I do
I will never be as exceptional
Exceptional as them

The thing is
I can be my own little shining star
Shining more ambitiously than them all
Showing what I can do
Best to wing the gifts I've been given
Pushing myself up above the clouds
Above all the stars
Until I rise up
One of the greatest of them all
Displaying me
Not perfect
Not normal
But happy little me

I hide how I feel
I can't hide that
I lie
Not bad lies
But ones that build up
Eventually bringing me down
I hide everything with laughs and smiles
It can be hard
I feel a hole within me with everything
It overflows

Tears
Cries
Emptiness

I try to make others happy, smile
Smile more than they thought
To see blissfulness in their faces
Losing their despondency
That's what makes me smile.

Sonja de Ferrars (12)
Bennett Memorial Diocesan School, Culverden Down

Pain Of The Game

In the rain, washed away
All the pain
But the voices are rising
No point running away
No point in hiding
Louder, stronger
Ringing, singing, beginning
Trying to speak out
To ask for help
But the sound never comes
You're broken, alone, just a token
You're okay, you're fine, no one can know what's inside
The drilling, blood-curdling
Heart erupting, with nothing,
Just the pain of the game you're stuck playing.

Penny Brown (12)
Bennett Memorial Diocesan School, Culverden Down

Extinction

So many animals are becoming extinct
So now it's time for us to think
What can we do to change this situation
Before it goes too far
More and more animals are going each day
We might now have to pray
If the animals go
Less and less food for us to eat
Animals deserve to live
We are the problem, why the creatures are going
First dodos
Now might be elephants as well
This has to stop
Before the end is yet to come.

Aryana Nedjati Gilani (11)
Bennett Memorial Diocesan School, Culverden Down

Confident

C onfidence is the ability to be brave

O nly you can make you feel weak

N o one should feel ashamed even though...

F inding your place is hard to beat

I nside yourself you will find that

D ifferences create identity

E veryone is like a superhero with their incredible mind

N ow you know that you have the power to be confident about your personality

T rust the confidence inside you.

Lily Goman
Bennett Memorial Diocesan School, Culverden Down

The Bully

Bullying is like a slow death
It swallows you, eats you up and tries to break and fade you
Even if you scream for help
No one will find you
Bullying turns the mirror to a voice
The mirror makes too much noise
Soon you crawl up into a ball and stay silent
One day it starts to feel violent
Every day seems like a battle and an effort.

Sianna Cunha (11)
Bennett Memorial Diocesan School, Culverden Down

Animal Rights

If we use our voices they could have freedom,
Not having a voice isn't a sign they want to go blind,
Burning their skin with perfume and foundation is just not right,
Freedom tastes nice to us but they will never relate,
Cages upon cages of scared little rabbits wondering if they will ever hop safely again.

Eliza Kassim (12)

Bennett Memorial Diocesan School, Culverden Down

It's Okay To Be Yourself

Don't pretend to be someone who you're not
Don't pretend to be someone who you aspire to be
Don't pretend to be someone who you like a lot
Don't feel you need to hide your identity
Because you amaze me in every single way
So don't let someone mean make you hide away.

Ethan Armstrong (12)
Bennett Memorial Diocesan School, Culverden Down

The Power Of Books

The struggle of life
The pain of people
The hardships of this world
But what of another?
A world of stories
Found by diving into a book
An escape, a relief
The embracing light that gives hope.

Isaac Delaney (12)
Bennett Memorial Diocesan School, Culverden Down

The Power Within

We are envious of our peers and what they can do,
But we must all remember that with age comes wisdom and
we'll get there too.
We thrive for perfection, flawlessness above all,
We never want to be wrong.
We don't listen to the power of failing, instead we see our
limitations as a roof.
Our next generation shall conquer the nation.

We have weaknesses, but that only defines us as human.
Our aspirations give us strength,
Our uniqueness defines us as superhuman.
What the future has in store for us we don't comprehend,
Even in dark times we always find a friend.

We see our ancestors as our influences, but we too shall get
there one day.
We might be recognised but that's not important.
Our notion when doing a deed should not be for fame, but
of what change it will bring fifty years from today.

There is a difference between 'human' and 'humane'.
'Human' means us physically, our mortal form.
'Humane' means something different: to be compassionate
and kind.
We all have rotten bits that we must endure,
But we can change how we look at the world through the
eyes of our strengths which are an immortal storm.

If we think about what our best selves are we will reach a zenith from which no one can bring us down.
Our aspirations are like climbing Mount Everest.
The journey is fatiguing and not temperate,
However, when heading to the top we know it was worth it as we feel the enthrallment, your latest adventure.
Our power is not our status,
It is not our firm fate,
Our past is the qualities that we enforce
And to get far in life, we must choose the power of Believing.

Karina Bradean (13)

Blaise High School, Henbury

Flying

She holds her head high, up to the sky
Looks the sun in the eye and dares to defy
The rules that were written
Written for her, you, I
She sees a challenge ahead and isn't scared to try
Because she's a teacher, a leader, born to fly
Born to touch the stars and live in the sky
She spends her days reaching her goals with a smirk in her eye
Her passion is high, high up
Among the clouds, not coming down
But she's not rushing to get there
However desperate she seems
Because she knows if she tries slowly, carefully, it'll be more than her dreams
Her dreams are of change, the dare to right the world
To follow her soul, reach her goal, despite what she's told
To change the whole world and teach it to fly
And she wants to spread her message far and wide
That it's enough to try
If you dare to defy your limits
And push the boundaries up to the sky
So you should climb the ladder knowing you could fall any time
But not be afraid to show the world you can cry
Because the whole world sees you break, sees you fall down

The emotion enough to make you feel drowned
Yet she's always there telling you don't you dare frown
To have another go
And to show the whole wide world that if you keep on trying
Soon you find in the sky you are flying.

Josephine Baker (14)
Bottisham Village College, Bottisham

Perception

In a way, everyone is blinded
Like a moth to a lamp, pinpointed and obsessed,

You meet a person for the first time,
Through an image of cracked glass,
Some shards clear, others incomprehensible,
Fogged up, clouded and jagged.

You see, greying hair or golden strands,
Wrinkled palms or dwarfish hands,
A crooked hunchback,
A stunted form.
You see, an outer shell or a first impression.
Who are they? Really.
That elderly man down the road, or that toddler next door.
Who are they? Really.
Old and young, wise and foolish.
Who are they... really?

Detached and severed,

"They're a prodigy,
an anomaly to a majority,
to a generation of senseless and trivial children,"

Wise beyond their years,

What is the standard?

I know what they're like at that age,
young and oblivious:
Naive to the world.

I know what they're like at that age
ignorant and selfish:
The world, running away from their frail grasp.

Really?

Was that perception always there?
From the dawn of your conception,
To the joining of your organisation,
Information and miscommunication,
Deception and a poor connection,

Will you be the exception to a societal infection?

Oliver Bayne (12)
Bottisham Village College, Bottisham

The Boy

There once was a boy
With a different face
His parents were poor
At school, he was a disgrace

He was always alone
He had no friends
No new things
No new trends

Bullied all day
He was always clowned
He was suffocating
But then he was found

He stood up for himself
They all heard him speak
And they all realised
That he was weak

They all apologised
They all felt bad
But that one bully
Just felt mad

The bully was angry
The boy stood strong
The bully was threatened
They stared for long

You see
Many of you may be stuck
But stand up for yourself
And you'll be in luck

The bully that you see
The bully that you fear
He is scared
Paranoid to hear you cheer

The bully sees potential in you
Which is why you are chosen
He is worried for what you can do
So overthrow them

Show them your strength
Show you're not afraid
Because I know
You are brave

There's nothing wrong with you
They just can't accept
That life redirects.

Inaam Hoque (14)
Bottisham Village College, Bottisham

Trust?

Trust, is this... trust?
It hurt what you did, a sword through my heart
The ocean in my eyes.
Like the roaring banshees of regret, of fear,
Tormenting me.
The screams are getting louder
Trust me
Louder!
I won't leave you
Louder!
I'm your friend
Together
Forever

Silence... I'm... alone?
All this time screaming for it to go away,
But now the emptiness flows in, leaving me and my head.
Alone.
Trust
Trust...
...Darkness

My eyes flicker open
The trust sets in, my hope is back
My life is back
Trust is a real thing, a thing you hold,

The thing you cherish.
Better days will come, all eclipses end then you can live again,
Then you can care and regain the trust.
I won't forgive you but I will never fully forget you.
My wound you can't see but it takes time to heal.
Actions have consequences, that statement is way too real.
Healing takes time, work and dedication
But friends and family are a good medication.
The hope will come, the light I see,
Things will get better, I promise
Trust me.

Kitty Van Nielen (12)
Bottisham Village College, Bottisham

The Top Three

Cristiano Ronaldo, not R9
Put in the effort,
Put in the time,
His dad was an alcoholic
But his son has never had a gin and tonic
Cleanest man on Earth
He also trains his son on the Astroturf

This is what we need
In this modern life
A diamond in the rough
A bit of sacrifice
A bit of bite
We need more GOATs like him
However, not better than Messi

Pelé, those 1,000 goals not on telly
Three World Cups
In his cabinet
Now that's what I call luck
Sorry, talent
See what's achievable
It's incredible
Hard work and determination

Number ten on his shirt
Then moved to Paris
Now number ten times three
Yes, it's Messi
Best youngster in the world
At the time
Could dribble through crowds in a straight line

All these three players
Don't you see
How well they've played
How well they've trained
Stay dedicated to the grind
And don't hold back

The biggest sport in the world
Owned by a few
Will see no one like him.

Leo Ingall (13)

Bottisham Village College, Bottisham

Self-Love

Self-love,
Appreciation for your spiritual growth,
Is this what you call self-love?
It is to be you, understand yourself and take care of your
own needs,
Why is this thing, this thing you call self-love, so important?
A small attitude like this creates and paves a path to being
more positive in life,
Being more successful in life,
Being more loved in life,
Other people are creating your standards,
Standards that you probably think you can't reach,
You think it's better for the others to like you,
So you change yourself,
You change your health,
And you try to be better than anyone else,
It's okay to be you,
It's okay to not change,
It's okay to judge yourself,
But please, pick yourself back up,
Learn to love yourself,
Learn to love yourself before you love anyone else,
Self-love is confidence,
Self-love is importance,
And self-love is to love yourself for who you really are,
Let self-love be your guidance.

Anna-Maria Wong (13)
Bottisham Village College, Bottisham

Be Yourself

You see people and want to be them,
See yourself as non-important
Want to change and be them
And then look back at yourself
And doubt yourself
Thinking that you should go into a shadow
And be what people think is 'cool'
What is cool?
Being yourself is the best self
Be yourself and everyone will respect you
People who made you doubt yourself are just jealous
And wish they were you!

Y ou can do whatever you want to do
O ur different thoughts make us special
U nderneath, inside, our different ideas bring us closer
R elish difference - if we all were the same we could never
be who we want to be
S o let's celebrate that and never put anyone down
E njoy being how you want to be - not what other people
want you to be
L ove yourself and do you
F riends, though different, are our best sort of power!

Don't be an image, be yourself,
Then everyone will follow?

Ella Deaton (12)
Bottisham Village College, Bottisham

We Are Who We Are

Some days are good, some are bad
We're not all the same
That's okay
We're all different in
Size and shape and personality.

I've had enough of all the haters
But we need to stand up to them
Let them know we're also here
It's fine to be different
And to be scared.

We're bisexual, gay
And also lesbian
That's what's good about us
We're like apples
All different
And I love that.

We're all equal
But don't get me wrong
We're only equal
Because we're people
Personality is always different.

Do you remember the
Time of your life
The memories you have
The best days you have
If not that's okay
It just means you're
Different.

If you're depressed
Or anxious and sad
Try to relax or be
Who you are
They're not your friend
If they don't accept you.

Philip Bilewski (12)
Bottisham Village College, Bottisham

Robots And Plastic

I see the girls standing there,
Short skirts and fake tans everywhere.
Always give people dark stares
But expect niceness in return.

Show their bodies on Instagram
(Of course applying filters to them).
Set unrealistic goals for girls
With their tiny waist and cute face.

All insecurities fly out the window,
Reducing individuality.
Only robots can be seen
From here to the corner of the Earth.

Real people stick out like a sore thumb
As filters aren't seen.
Self-esteem plummets again
And hope for humanity as well.

But once in a while, a human comes around.
With insecurities, no filter and modest clothes.
My heart lights up but dulls again
As people shun her out for not being like them.

I see the girls standing there
Short skirts and fake tans everywhere.
Removing those in society
Who aren't as plastic as they are.

Lauryn Koyi (16)
Bottisham Village College, Bottisham

Blank

Everyone is unique
Everyone is different
Whether it be race, face
Or the memories you have

No one starts with all their memories
But we gain them differently
It could be from holidays or special occasions
But these are just a few

Our lives are like a blank canvas
Our memories and experiences like the brush
Painting our identity like an artist paints a masterpiece
But for some people, a masterpiece is too much

This is okay as everyone is different
Unique through passions and memories
Everyone starts life as a canvas
We choose how to paint the blank canvas

Don't feel that you can't
Feel like you are the superhero
Embrace your confidence
Don't feel you are worth zero

Everyone is unique
Don't feel ashamed of yourself
Control your life the way you want to
You control your canvas.

Zach Holder (12)

Bottisham Village College, Bottisham

Social Media

Let's talk about social media
We all hide behind our screens
Hiding from ourselves, the people around us
People set standards, rules, opinions
So much that when we step back into reality
We don't know who we are anymore
We feel uncomfortable in our bodies
We gaze into the mirror and wonder
Why aren't I like them?
Why don't I look like them?
We feel so bad, we slip back into the false reality
And the cycle repeats again
And again... and again
Let's talk about social media
The way it changes us
Brings out the other sides to people
The way we shame others for being honest
Or for sharing the things they love
But then there's the people who care
The people who take their time to help others
To make them laugh
And yet they get no recognition
Let's talk about social media
Or let's not.

Grace Gaskin (13)
Bottisham Village College, Bottisham

A Letter To My Future Self

Relax, don't stress,
Right now I am working hard at school,
Stressed like a heart surgeon,
Worried about what my exam results will be,

When you are reading this you will be settled down,
A strong job that gives you enough money for a living,
Kids and a partner,
Relaxing by the swimming pool in Spain,
Lucky you,

At this point in time,
My parents, my teachers,
Plan everything for me,
They are responsible for me,
And care for me,

My future self will be responsible for themselves
And others, like kids and animals,

So don't be all relaxed and peaceful,
But just remember to sometimes take a deep breath in,
And remember you are the boss, the person of the house.

So remember, relax, don't stress
And be yourself.

Sasha Elsden (11)
Bottisham Village College, Bottisham

Speak Up

Look
Just look around
Look up from your device
At all the world and all the ground

The school bell rings
And it's time to go home

You think back on your day
Everything is dull and blue
This feeling of negativity, nothing new

The school bullies pushed and shoved
Or perhaps they mocked you for who you loved
They take your mind and twist and turn it
The right they have to make you this way they have not
earnt it

You want to speak out
But you fear for the worst
This horrible feeling
Like a curse
Maybe it's best just to leave it alone
But if you do, it will only prolong

Speak up, for we cannot read your mind
If there is something bugging you
Tell us what is on your mind

For we can help you, no matter what
If you don't tell us this feeling will not stop.

Kaitlyn Hudson (14)

Bottisham Village College, Bottisham

Life Before Death

Don't worry about death
It will get you nowhere
Enjoy life while it's there
You only get one try
So don't spend it with a tear in your eye

Push yourself to your limits
Help others who might feel down
But don't do it wearing a frown
Start a family
Don't be a bore

And when you're feeling down
Get rid of that frown
Turn it upside down

Collect those good memories
'Cause you'll want them when it's your time to go
But do not cry
When it's your turn to say goodbye
And don't let it get you down
Don't flip that frown around
Just remember the good times
'Cause you're here and it's wonderful
So enjoy your life
Hold on tight to those good times
You're lucky to be here

So don't be sad
Instead, be very glad.

Billy Turner (14)
Bottisham Village College, Bottisham

Memories

Splash, splash, splash,
Sprinkles of water in the air,
Cry, cry, cry,
Water fight,
Cry, cry, cry,
Fall over,
Cry, cry, cry.

You're it,
Ha, ha, ha,
Chasing you,
Run faster,
Faster, faster, faster,
You can't get me,
Ha, ha, ha,
Hurry up,
Before you lose,
Ha, ha, ha.

You're stuck,
You can't get me,
You're stuck,
I am free,
You're stuck,
Under I go,
Both of you are stuck.

It's my first day,
Too tall,
Too small,
Scary,
Test,
Too scary,
I am going to fail,
Save me,
Help,
Too scary.

It's the holiday,
I can't wait to see family,
Party,
Wow, wow, wow,
Let's have fun,
Yay,
I've got the best thing coming up,
Yay.

Elizabeth Johns (12)
Bottisham Village College, Bottisham

Sleep

Sleep is good
You will be relaxed
Cherish it while you can
You might never get it again

You might get insomnia
And daydream about sleep
You will spend hours trying to sleep
Those hours get longer, turning to days and months

You might even forget what sleep is
And only have it as a distant memory
You might forget what sleep is and what life was like before
it
Then you might not be with us

As I said before
Sleep while you can
Don't be scared to sleep
Nothing can hurt you

You may get scared of nightmares
But if you don't get your sleep
Those nightmares will be there
In your waking state

So stay relaxed
And sleep
Because the next one
May be your last.

Aidan Williamson (12)
Bottisham Village College, Bottisham

Head To Toe

You're beautiful,
Your hair,
Your body,
Your face.

The scrolling that never stops,
The people in the street,
The non-stop bullying,
Can interfere lots.

"Chubby"
"Skeleton"
"Terrorist"
"Ugly"
Don't let it get in your head.

You get wound up,
So insecure,
Just sitting and crying in bed.

But all of you,
Head to toe,
Is stunning,
Nonetheless.

The stretch marks tell a story,
Hair makes you stand out,
Beautiful face, so unique,
No matter smile or pout.

Love yourself for who you are,
Because I don't think you know,
You're absolutely gorgeous,
From your head to your toes.

Tilly Fry (12)
Bottisham Village College, Bottisham

Your Personality

Who am I?
Who are you?
Are we ugly?
Are we pretty?
Are we fat?
Are we skinny?
Are we good enough?
Are we worth it?
Who are you?
Who am I?

Your hair colour,
Your skin colour,
Your religion,
Your past,
Your sexuality,
Does not reflect your personality.

They're probably jealous
Of how wonderful you are
So block out the bad
And reach for the stars
Reach for your dreams
Never give up
On what you want to be
Your personality is who you are

Don't worry about your appearance
Just focus on your actions.

No one is perfect
Everyone has flaws
If someone says you're not good enough
Just ignore.

We are amazing!

Paige Denston (12)
Bottisham Village College, Bottisham

If I Met My Future Self

If I met my future self,
Maybe they'd tell me that everyone is equal
That all lives matter
That it doesn't matter if you're black or white
Gay or straight
Girl or boy.

If I met my future self,
Maybe they'd tell me that there was no more war
No more fighting
No more evacuating
No more pain and suffering.

If I met my future self,
Maybe they'd tell me that people were fighting more
important battles
Like cancer
Like the climate crisis
Like finding cures and saving people

If I met my future self,
Maybe they'd tell me that I made a difference
That I campaigned to make everyone equal
That I helped to stop the wars
That I helped fight more important battles.

Thea Burgess (12)
Bottisham Village College, Bottisham

Motivation

A day of joy,
A day of pain,
Two days of joy,
Two days of pain,
The pain may cloud
But the joy makes us proud.

The light of joy will always prevail,
Over the darkness of pain and betrayal,
The mind is our mail,
Our favourites stay and prosper,
But the worst makes its way to the rubbish bin.

Don't wait until another year,
Rather finish by the end of the year,
The rainy days are forgettable,
Warm days are the ones we remember,
The negativity will always lose,
As the positivity will shine bright,
But always remember.

A day of joy,
A day of pain,
Two days of joy,
Two days of pain,
The pain may cloud,
But the joy makes us proud.

Leo Saunders (12)
Bottisham Village College, Bottisham

Every Day Is A New Day

Every day is a new day
Cherish it like your last
Spend the time you have wisely
Doing what you love

Every day is a new day
Try something new
Are you going to?

Every day is a new day
Be safe in what you do
Protect your loved ones
As they will do the same for you

Every day is a new day
Be kind, helpful and caring
Help ones who need to be helped
As one day that could be you

Every day is a new day
Be you
Embrace who you are
Take time for you

Every day is a new day
Try the best in everything you do
Because when you achieve
You feel empowered

Every day is a new day
And a second chance
Take a deep breath
And start again.

Cara Thompsett (12)

Bottisham Village College, Bottisham

The Darkness

It used to terrify me,
Used to eat my thoughts alive,
Hit that switch and run!
Darkness, never my friend,
Darkness, there until the end...

Everywhere, under my bed,
My toes tucked in the covers,
My head under the pillow,
"Go away!" I said.

My heart thumping out of my chest,
It's coming for me,
I can hear it creeping up the stairs,
Darkness, never my friend,
Darkness, there until the end...

Be careful,
Hide before it comes,
You're lucky if you're quick enough,
To dive into your bed.
It's friends with the devil,
And it's driving you round the bend.
Darkness, never my friend,
Darkness, there until the end.

Alex Challis (12)
Bottisham Village College, Bottisham

Dear Future Me

In the future, I imagine me as a rich actress,
Strutting into the Met Gala, making an entrance.
My life would have much more rest.

Every day I wake up, go to school, have dinner and repeat.
Wake up, school, have dinner, always the same dull street.

Maybe if I do something about it, I won't have to be so bored,
Like a blacksmith melting and reshaping a sword.

Maybe I should wait, or maybe I should go,
Stop for the red light or break the law.

Well, dear future me,
I hope I could be
Much more than I am now.

Despite all my flaws,
I can rise up through it all.

So dear future me,
I hope I can be
The best and fantastic, wonderful me.

Amelia Koyi (12)
Bottisham Village College, Bottisham

Future Self

Dear future self,
Come on,
You can do it,
You can achieve it.
Try your hardest and work through it
Whatever you do,
Whenever you do,
You can achieve your dreams.

Try, try, try and
Fry, fry, fry your eggs.
You shine,
You rock,
Full of joy,
Full of toys.

Sit back and relax,
You're as good as your mom,
Complete your tasks,
And buy your flasks.
Do your best,
See your best,
Try your best.

Go over what you can achieve
See what you can achieve
You can do anything

Anything you want
Just remember when you were little
You never gave up
So
Today is your day to shine.

Nisha Dant (12)
Bottisham Village College, Bottisham

Who Knows?

Maybe you think you look fine,
Maybe you think you are fine,
Maybe people say they like you,
Maybe people say they hate you,
But one thing is certain: we are all human.
If we are all human we are all one,
Maybe with different hair colour, eyes,
Maybe even disabilities,
Maybe you suffer,
Maybe you don't
We all have our mental health,
Our physical health,
If people have been harmful to you,
Stand up for yourself,
Don't let people define you,

You are more than your past, don't let it control you,
Keep your head up, you can't save everyone,
If need you help,
Reach out,
Don't let people define you.

Dominic George (13)
Bottisham Village College, Bottisham

We Are All Different

We are all different,
Some people have brown hair,
Others blonde, black, ginger,
Some people have dark skin
Some people have light skin.

Some people have curly hair, wavy, straight
Some people are fat, skinny, in the middle
Some people have size six feet
Some size five, four, three.

We are all different, unique, normal.
Some of us aren't normal
What is normal?
Is it to be fat, size three feet, curly brown hair?
Is it to be skinny, size six feet, straight blonde hair?

Normal doesn't exist, average, but not normal.
We are all different, like snowflakes
We all have at least one thing making us
Different.

India Uchekwo (12)
Bottisham Village College, Bottisham

Dear Past Me

Dear past me,
Be who you want to be
Accept that not everyone will like you for who you are
But know that the ones who truly love you are the only ones
that matter
Do not let your anxiety
Define who you want to be
Don't let anybody bring down a beautiful, shining star
You are who you are...

Some days have, and still will be hard on you
But you'll be alright, just keep pushing through
Your mistakes and bad days have made me who I am today
and
Although they've been difficult for me
I have coped and I'm still okay
You may be told that you're not good enough
But keep holding your head high, stay strong, be tough!

Naomi Ghevaert (12)
Bottisham Village College, Bottisham

Football, A Dream

Football, a dream
Football, an escape
Football, a team
Football, the freedom, the enjoyment, the shape
Ronaldo and Messi
Rooney and Drogba
Football, the GOATs
Football, take notes
Football, work hard
Football, the love, the passion, don't get a red card
Maradona and Pelé
Mbappe and Haaland
Football, the lifestyle
Football, go the extra mile
Football, live the life
Football, the money, the fame, but you must stay nice
Neymar and Griezmann
Kane and Benzema
For football, you have to push
Struggle and fall
To come from nothing and have the dream
You must first be willing to sacrifice it all.

Thomas Beaven (14)
Bottisham Village College, Bottisham

What Is Normal?

How do you define normal? You can't
Impossible
Everybody is different, that's good though
You could be a baker, creator,
Scientist, surfer, chef, anything
You can try to be normal
Impossible

Everybody is different
Everybody looks different, sounds different
Speaks different
It's good
You could be a police officer
Nurse, farmer, waitress, doctor
Everybody's different
But in some ways similar
Kindness, unity, happiness, love, joy

If you're good at heart
You'll be treated fairly
Corruption
Disruption
Separates us
Deep in the heart love keeps
Us strong.

Toby Armer (12)
Bottisham Village College, Bottisham

This Is Me

This is me, one, two, three,
I want to be,
The one to make my family proud,
Shed a few tears,
I want to be known to get away fears,
Be a good person,
Loyal, true and trustworthy,
I am Christian and proud of my ways,
I promise to live my life with pride and joy,
After all, I am a boy,
Let me dream,
I want to beam to the top with grit,
When I play football I want to let my family relax and see
their kid succeed,
That's the future I hope to see,
When it comes to life my mum's most important,
When she's happy I'm joyful,
When she's sad I cry,
If I make it,
It's for her,
This is me.

Kayden Bidwell (12)
Bottisham Village College, Bottisham

Just Keep Going

When you feel like it's all gone down
When you want to smile but you have to frown
Keep on going and persevere
Lead with courage and not fear
Shine your light and let them see
Instead of flying away like a bumblebee
Be a leader and stand out from the crowd
Being a leader means you need to be proud
Lead like a lion ahead of its team
To inspire people and give them a dream
To be empowered you need to be brave
To help everybody in your style and save

Keep going, keep going, keep going
Let your brave mind keep flowing
Have a mind and heart of steel
To help homeless people have a meal.

Benjamin Robinson (12)
Bottisham Village College, Bottisham

A Gift And A Curse

My family can be a gift,
My family can be a curse.
Whether it is my sister denying access to the bathroom,
Or my brother breaking my Lego,
I should love them no matter what happens.

My pets can be a gift,
My pets can be a curse.
Whether it is my fish committing cannibalism,
Or my dog chewing up my mum's slippers,
I should care for them and love them no matter what
happens.

My life can be a gift,
My life can be a curse.
When it is my darkest hour someone is there,
Or in a moment of great triumph, there is someone to share
it with,
They love me no matter what happens.

Jack Brandt (12)
Bottisham Village College, Bottisham

What Is Life?

What is life?
An orb of happiness and joy
An endless spiral of sadness and depression
A ticking time bomb of death and the end
Something to treasure, love and protect
Something to make the most of and
Learn something new
Make a name for yourself
Be proud to be you
And at the end of the day, there is something you need to
know
You're at the wheel of your boat
Trying to keep everything afloat
The sea can be choppy
The sea can be calm
But if you get through the ups and the downs
And you've had a good time
You've done a good job and you've found your treasure.

Jacob Hubbard (12)
Bottisham Village College, Bottisham

You Are Limitless

The sky seems so far away
Too far to ever reach, huh?
You'll reach and reach but just don't stop
Don't look down or be scared at the drop
You could fall and fall, just hang onto something
Don't cushion yourself with nothing
Live without regrets
They're the biggest threat
To falling back down to the ground

People say the sky is the limit
I say go a bit further
Reach for the stars
It's not that far
Will yourself to do it
Until you're up in the sun's orbit
Don't look behind you
Better days will find you
Just go for it.

Violet Martin (12)
Bottisham Village College, Bottisham

What Do You Want To Be?

What do you want to be?
Do you want to be a true friend?
Do you want to be a real fighter?
Do you want to listen to no one but your heart?
You can feel like who you want to be
And that is me

If you could be anything what would you be?
A cop, a vet, a doctor, anything you want
To anything from your imagination to your world
You can be anything

Do you want to be hard-working?
Do you want to be kind?
Do you want to feel safe?
Well, no one else cares what you are
Or what you want to be
It doesn't matter what you like
Or who you like
Just be!

Dylan Pilgrim (12)
Bottisham Village College, Bottisham

Never Stop Believing

What are your hopes?
Your dreams? Your ambitions?
Do you know them?

We all want difference,
And maybe a change,
But are we all ready?
Are we willing to make a change?
Are you ready to stand up for your rights?

Your hopes, dreams and ambitions,
The differences and changes we will make,
They're yours, and nothing can stand in your way,
Only if you're willing to do anything and everything

Face facts, persevere, thrive through this,
You will get there,
Just never give up on what you desire,

Stand strong and never stop believing!

Emily Parnell (11)
Bottisham Village College, Bottisham

Hello

Hello,
Hello you,
How do you do?
How are you feeling?
I'm feeling good too,
How was your day?
A day is like a battle,
And you may not be able to stop battling,
But you can make every day a win,
So hello you,
How do you do?
Hope you're feeling well,
How was your day?
Was it swell?
I know this is supposed to be empowering,
And I may not be feeling well,
But I do wish you the best in the future,
For you and your future self,
So hello,
Hello you,
I hope you're feeling well,
How was your day?
I hope it was swell.

Elliot Rye
Bottisham Village College, Bottisham

Live

As bullets whizz past my head
Please remember to enjoy everything

That first kiss that you can never take back
Or that time you spoke to your mates

Because trust me, you can't take them back

Enjoy the fights and arguments
Embrace the losses then build off them
Work hard - education is key

Because trust me, you don't want to be like me

The people that support you
Support them back
Please do it for me
I may not last long
But you will

Don't waste it
Remember you're lucky
You're not like me.

Liam Dunham (12)
Bottisham Village College, Bottisham

LGBTQ

They look at us weird sometimes when we tell them,
They might say we are sinners,
But we know we are not,
But why do they say this?

They tell us to change,
But they know we can't,
So many of us in this world are part of this community.

Why can't you see that your words affect us
So badly even if you didn't mean to?
If you did mean to we will come back stronger,
Why are they like this?

We stand as one,
We are stronger together,
We are the LGBTQ+ community,
And we are stronger together,
We are stronger than you.

Molly Swift (12)
Bottisham Village College, Bottisham

Lost At Sea

Dear past me,
I know you will feel lost at sea,
Like you're alone,
Like you want to flee,
The harsh waves of society won't stop crashing against the land,
But you need to stand tall,
Even when you feel like you are sinking into the sand,
As the sea washes over you,
You'll be the one to float,
Hold your loved ones close,
And always sail your own boat.

As the storm fades away,
The sun comes out,
You will feel the strength,
No more doubt,
Raise your sail,
Set off to sea,
No more anchors,
You are free.

Louisa Gordon (14)
Bottisham Village College, Bottisham

Smothered

Burning in its own heat
Smothered by a blanket
The riots grow bigger
The peace grows smaller
It cries for help
We know what's wrong
But society has grown lazy
Pretending the problems aren't there
The roar of protests
The rage of the few people
To be listened to by who?
The critics who cause these problems
They don't care until it affects them
It cries for help
So close to saving
So close to help
It is too late now
Soon we will be burning in our own heat
Smothered by the Earth's forever warming blanket.

Felix Agar (14)
Bottisham Village College, Bottisham

The Lesson Of Love

Heartbreak,
Try not to go through it,
Stress, sadness, guilt, pressure, anger, pain,
That's not the way of love,
Love isn't some game
You can't just play around with it,
Love is a person, thing, anything you dream,
Love is something you admire,
You can love your pet, family, or even that one person,
Love is a mystery,
Love is a book, you could start the next chapter,
Love isn't compulsory,
You don't have to go through it,
Be cautious about love,
Because you never know what's in the dark.

Courtney Parker (12)
Bottisham Village College, Bottisham

Dear Future Me

Dear future me,
How do I progress?
Do I pass the GCSE tests?
What's my life like?
Do I get the house of my dreams
And ride in fancy limousines?
Do I spend my days working with actors,
Winning best actress, eating Michelin-star lobsters?

Dear future me,
Am I famous?
Can I afford the nicest dresses?
Will I appear on live shows and tell them my confessions?
What I do makes me happy
Because it's not just about the money
It's about showing other people you can do it
No matter what.

Matilda Malagueira-Cockman (12)

Bottisham Village College, Bottisham

The Man And The Turtle

The man sat down
Just by the shore
But he wondered
What this was for

The turtle floated
Just by the sand
Only to ask for a helping hand

The man saw the turtle
And smiled with glee
He walked down the shore
And thought, *yippee!*

The turtle was scared
Afraid and under the light
He hid inside his shell
With so much fright

The man said
Don't be afraid, I won't hurt you
The turtle's fins came out
And decided to welcome him too!

Aiden Laws (12)
Bottisham Village College, Bottisham

Pretty Girls On Social Media

You see these pretty figured girls online
Waiting for them to be you

Watching these girls on your phone
Wishing you were them
Watching for days and days for it to be you

Standing there in the mirror
Feeling helpless, worthless
Standing there wishing you would get prettier

Trying to get slimmer
Just so you can be their body shape
No, you are perfect just the way you're born to be

Online is like a deep black hole
A deep hole
So please don't fall in deep.

Isla Beech (12)
Bottisham Village College, Bottisham

I Am Me

I am me,
I aspire to be whoever I want to be,
Although people might not want me to be,
I am me.

People might want me to be,
Someone who is not me,
Do not take that vision,
Be who you want to be.

A dream of what you want to be,
Is only an opportunity for you to grab and change me.

This is all a dream,
An image of who you want to be,
Take that opportunity,
And put your mind to it,
Pursue that dream.

I am me,
And I love who I have become to be.

Poppy Banks (12)
Bottisham Village College, Bottisham

Self-Confidence

You are amazing
You are worth it
You are strong
Come on, just believe in yourself
You've got this
Just believe
Breathe... it will be okay

What makes you happy?
Where is your safe place?
Imagine you're there
Happy, feeling safe and loving life
Now... whenever you feel like you're not worth it or anything like that
Imagine you're there
In your safe place

It's okay to not feel okay
But you have to remember
People love you
For you.

Lily Ison (12)
Bottisham Village College, Bottisham

Believe In Yourself

People might discourage you,
They might say rumours about you,
They might make up sad conversations,
Make you feel worried, threatened or frightened.

Don't listen to their words,
Let those words and phrases fly away from you,
Bring your ambition and achievement to life,
Bring enjoyment and happiness.

Work hard,
Don't give up,
Let the world hear you,
Listen to yourself and gain your goals.

Be a role model to others,
Love yourself,
No pain, no gain!

Prathana Jeyathas (12)
Bottisham Village College, Bottisham

Perfect

Social media makes your life like a filter,
It makes you want to be someone who's not you,
Hate, body shame,
It makes you look like a dull blank canvas with no meaning,
No concept,
But really you hide a natural beauty,
Full of bright colours and confidence,
So go and be the brightest star that you already are,
Be the person you were born to be,
Not the person that other people built,
You are perfect,
And no one can ever change that,
And don't let anyone tell you otherwise.

Isabel Parnell (11)
Bottisham Village College, Bottisham

Ambitions

They could be close,
They could be far,
Your mind might be set,
Your mind might be free,

You might not think it's possible,
You might want to give up,
Maybe you feel confident,
Maybe you don't,

Don't give up on yourself,
Don't underestimate yourself,
You're more than you think,
Your confidence is priceless,

Try to work hard,
Try to believe in yourself,
Make sure you're kind,
And make sure you're adventurous.

Samuel Grimwade (12)
Bottisham Village College, Bottisham

Imagine

Imagine
A life full of peace
A happy ending
No war but love and happiness
Imagine
No racism
No hate
Empathy
Imagine
A life full of peace
A happy ending
No war but love and happiness
Imagine
No homophobia
No prejudice
No sexism
Why?
Why do we live like this?
Always arguing
Never agreeing
All we need is compassion
Imagine
A life full of peace
A happy ending

No war but love and happiness
Just imagine...

Holly Hromek (12)
Bottisham Village College, Bottisham

You're A Natural Beauty

Social media makes your life like a filter,
Makes you want to be someone you're not,
Hate,
Body shaming,
Bullying,
Makes you feel like a dull blank canvas with no pretty
drawing on,
But really you are a natural beauty,
Full of bright colours and confidence,
So go and be the bright shining star that you already are,
You have the right to be one,
Ignore the hate,
Look in the mirror,
And embrace your natural beauty,
Because that's what you really are.

Connie Burling (11)
Bottisham Village College, Bottisham

Don't Be Sad

Don't spend your days,
Just thinking about bad things,
Don't be sad,
Think of good things,
Not the bad.

Make your life worth living,
Try not to be sad,
Make sure you're happy,
There's a whole world out there for you,
Do you really hate your life?

Don't spend life being sad,
Make sure you don't have sleepless nights,
They make things worse for you,
Make your life happy,
Don't be sad.

Tom Robinson (11)
Bottisham Village College, Bottisham

Relax And Enjoy Yourself

Relax on the sofa and watch TV,
You'll be okay,
Take a break and chill,
Do some Lego,
Watch Star Wars,
Read a book,
Research reptiles some more,

Play with your pets,
Watch Lord of the Rings,
Take a walk,
See your grandparents,
Play a game on the Xbox,
Go kayaking,
Talk to family,
Play on your phone,
See your friends,
Have fun and enjoy yourself,
You only have one life,
So make it count.

Edward Penfound (12)
Bottisham Village College, Bottisham

Lemons

Lemons are yellow
Lemons are round
Lemons are sweet
Lemons are sour
Lemons grow

Lemons are small
Lemons are large
Lemons are funny
Lemons are sad
Lemons feel

Lemons are old
Lemons are young
Lemons are rotting
Lemons are breathing
Lemons age

Lemons are kind
Lemons are smart
Lemons are empowered
Lemons learn

Lemons grow on a lemon tree,
Just like you and me.

Martha Houlder (12)
Bottisham Village College, Bottisham

Just Breathe

New year, new me
That's what I tell myself
I'm going to wake up early
I'm going to read every day
I'm going to exercise
I'm only eating healthily
I'm going to lose weight

Stop
No
Why do you do this to yourself?
What do you get out of this?
Nothing

It doesn't matter
Just take a break
You don't owe anyone anything
You need a rest
Just stop
Just breathe.

Audrey Hurles (11)
Bottisham Village College, Bottisham

Be Yourself

It's important to be yourself
Because people would love you
It's important to be yourself
So that people can see who you really are
Nobody should think they have the right
To treat you poorly because they don't
Love your culture and express it
Love the personality you have
And don't try to hide it
Be grateful for what you have
And don't compare yourself to others
And don't let others bring you down.

Zerrin Dhillon (14)
Bottisham Village College, Bottisham

Snowflakes

Snowflakes
They're different yet the same
Unique in ways no one imagines
Pushed and pushed towards beauty
Yet so far from perfection

Snowflakes
Some strong, some weak
But yet are still unique
Some picture perfect, some not
Camera shy and photogenic

Snowflakes
Some big, some small
Some are skinny, some chunky
Some have different patterns
And some are plain
Yet we are all unique.

Lee Fuller (14)
Bottisham Village College, Bottisham

It's The Darkness

It's black, it's dark
It's full of mysterious souls
You don't know what's there
It's full of secrets

As it patiently waits for you
You dread walking in
"Don't do it!" the scream in your head yells at you
You can't find the switch
You panic
Would it go away?
Nope

Maybe... just maybe...
It clicks and it creaks
The floor is squeaking
You walk in...

Evie Drew (12)
Bottisham Village College, Bottisham

Go! Go! Go!

You have got this!
You can do this!
If you want to achieve it
Then achieve it.

You have your whole life to live
But no one knows when it will end
So whatever you do
Do it with fun.

Go, go, go
Win, win, win
Try your hardest
And you will get in
Do it.

You have the power
So don't give up
Do your best
What is there to lose
And finally,
Win.

Isabel Arnott (12)
Bottisham Village College, Bottisham

Thinking About You

Roses are red
Violets are blue
My heart is dead
Thinking about you
Alone with my thoughts
Trapped in this head
I don't sleep at night
As I'm thinking about what you said
But your imperfections
Perfectly summed up
When you were with me
The voices were gone
They have come flooding back
So roses are red
Violets are blue
My heart will still always belong to you.

Honey-Rose Howard (13)
Bottisham Village College, Bottisham

Hot Destruction

Forests burning into ash,
Houses lit in flames,
Trees plummeting to the ground,
Bash! Everyone's suddenly afraid.

Animals losing their homes,
Struggling to survive,
Burning forests killing them all,
Lucky if they're alive.

Bright blue skies,
Turning into smoke,
Koalas endangered and alone,
Places no longer habitable,
No place for them to call home.

Emilia Clough (12)
Bottisham Village College, Bottisham

The Brighter Side

Look on the brighter side,
There's always a brighter side,
The light will shine through,
The light will be true.

Pierce through the dark lies,
The warm truth can't always hide,
Search through the darkness,
Until there's no darkness.

Don't cower and hide in fear,
Know the light is always near,
Look on the brighter side,
There's always a brighter side.

Walter Donnelly (12)
Bottisham Village College, Bottisham

Life's Too Short

You might go through a low point
But there's lots of time left to enjoy
When you feel low go and sit down
And take some deep breaths and just try to calm down
Go try new things like pet a dog or get some fresh air
To clear all the negative things out of your head
Change it all, your negativity to positivity
Go live your life, go have some brilliant experience
Life's too short to feel down!

Ellis Beech (12)
Bottisham Village College, Bottisham

You Are You

You see that person over there
You could be them
You could make the choices that they made
You could choose the path they dared to take
You could be the person that they are
But is that you?
Yes, you may look the same
Yes, you may have all the same
But under all that everyone can see
You are you
No one knows who you are until they peel away the skin and
see what is thriving deep within.

Imogen Swygart (13)
Bottisham Village College, Bottisham

The Dog In The Cage

Once, I saw this animal,
In a cage looking defeated.
I took a closer look,
And realised it was a dog.
Its fur in a shade of grey,
Its body weak and filthy.
No one took any notice of it,
But pity built up on me.
I wondered what it looked like
Before it ended up there.
Please, I beg you,
Treat animals better,
Treat them nicely
And you'll find them lovely.

Chloe Choi (11)
Bottisham Village College, Bottisham

Me

I am me
Filled with glee
You can call me emo or a Skittle
But me to you is just a riddle
Just because I'll like a woman
Doesn't mean you have to be stubborn
I dress the way I like
Can't change me
You may be hurtful to me
But I'll still be filled with glee
I am me
Filled with glee
Rarely will you ever see
Me not filled with glee.

Heather Cheryl-Rose Hutchison (12)
Bottisham Village College, Bottisham

Everyone's Different

Everyone's different and unique
Whatever your race
There will be someone
There for you

Don't be upset if you don't
Look like the person next to you
Everyone's human, everyone's different
Be proud, not worried or anxious

Everyone's beautiful in their own way
And there will be someone who
Likes you for who you are.

Xavier Brame (12)
Bottisham Village College, Bottisham

Keep Going

Keep walking, don't worry
You will be there soon
Just pick up a spoon
Eat breakfast
And soon a day has gone by
Time flies when you're happy
So keep going
And enjoy life
And as soon as you know it you'll be in year seven
With new worries
But like before, just keep going
And time will go by faster
As long as you're optimistic.

Ruby Chantelle Corner (12)
Bottisham Village College, Bottisham

Learn To Love Yourself

Don't let others bring you down
You are perfect the way you are
You shouldn't change yourself
To fit society's standards
Learn to love yourself.

Pictures in magazines are edited
Next time you pick up a magazine remember it's fake!
Don't believe that that's what you have to look like for
people to love you
Learn to love yourself.

Thea Brunton (12)
Bottisham Village College, Bottisham

Empowered

You are unique,
Special
And different.
You are the greatest you there is.
Be who you are,
Break through the bars
That hold you down.
You are brought to the world
To make a difference.
One small thing can make a change.
Be who you are
Don't change for anyone
Because you are unique
Special
And different
Like a snowflake.

Molly Clarke Stow (12)
Bottisham Village College, Bottisham

The Brighter Side

Always look on the bright side of life,
As the bad is worse,
Always look at the better things,
The bad is worse.

Good is better than bad,
Trust me on that,
It can turn on you and make you sad,
Trust me on that.

Always look on the brighter side of life,
The bad is worse,
Always look at the better things,
The bad is worse.

Rory Langdon (12)
Bottisham Village College, Bottisham

Motivate And Achieve

Don't give up, find a way around your problems
But if you can't, come back to it later
Believe in yourself, embrace challenges
Help others if they are struggling but don't judge them for it
Try and be the best possible version of yourself
Try to achieve your goals by motivating yourself
And motivate others to help them achieve their goals.

River Churchman (14)
Bottisham Village College, Bottisham

Nature Needs You

Join me,
Join us,
We can make a change,
We can make a difference,
We need help,
No, they need help,
And we can't hide anymore,
The world has no law.

We need to think before we act,
We need to leave the world intact,
Why don't we stop the war
And stop all the anger in the law?
Let's finish by the shore.

Dominic Ng'ang'a (12)
Bottisham Village College, Bottisham

Snowboarder

The coldness of the snow,
The shock of the ice,
The wind,
The fog,
I have never felt so alive.

The whispers of the trees,
The whistle of the board,
The thwump of the snow as I brake,
The jolt in my belly as I see the huge drop.

I take a deep breath,
I slide off the ledge,
Down,
Down,
Down.

Mateo Rodriguez Pariente (12)
Bottisham Village College, Bottisham

Why Is It Important To Be Yourself?

To be yourself is to be someone you are not expected to be
I create my own standards and own goals in life
I choose to be me, not her, not him, not them, and not you
I choose me

To be yourself is to be empowered
Your life is your life, empower it yourself
Choose to be you, not her, not him and not us
You choose you.

Freya Brown (13)
Bottisham Village College, Bottisham

Man U

Goal, goal
This is what we do
When we lose
We train harder
We are Man U
The greatest

We are the best
Five championships
That's right
You wonder how
When you know it's simple
Practice, practice
Practice
Whenever we fall
We get back up
Because
This is what we do.

Edward N Fernandes (12)
Bottisham Village College, Bottisham

Lovely Lemons

All lemons are special in their own way,
Some are small and some are big,
Some are bumpy and some are smooth,
Some are sour and some are sweet,
Some have lots of seeds and others only a few.
So just remember,
All lemons are special in their own way,
So most importantly
Don't let others get to you.

Olive Brown (12)
Bottisham Village College, Bottisham

Maddy

I had a dream,
About making music,
Everyone I cared for and loved,
Said that I should just leave it,

So I cried and sobbed,
All through the night,
Until I saw,
A star shining bright.

I stood there smiling,
Looking happy,
It was the one and only person,
My sister, Maddy.

Clarkson Mantlo (12)
Bottisham Village College, Bottisham

Today And The Future...

Today -
Stressed,
Sad,
Depressed,
Mad,
Behind on bills,
Lots of debt,
Feeling ill,
Have barely slept,
A severe headache,
Causing lots of pain,
Feels like drowning within a lake,
A migraine,
However,
There is a tomorrow,
But what will *you* do with it?

Beau O'Gorman (12)
Bottisham Village College, Bottisham

Kindness

Be kind to everyone no matter what,
Be kind to people with disabilities,
Be kind to people from different communities,
Be kind to people of different religions,

Be kind to all,
Be kind to people of different nationalities,
Be kind to people with different conditions,
Be kind to everyone.

Lucy Bridgeman (12)
Bottisham Village College, Bottisham

Who Is There?

Who is there?
The soul that lies in the dark
As quiet as a mouse but as bold as the sun in June
The silence, the sadness and the sorrow hangs in the air
Like a spider hanging from its web
Footsteps creeping across the room
Fingers wrapping around the door, itching to come in.

Florence Stannard (12)
Bottisham Village College, Bottisham

I Am Okay About Being Different

I am okay about being different
Having a disability
It's basically my ability
Sometimes I get really sad
But sometimes I get really mad
My mum is the best
She keeps me alive when I rest
I am the rock
I am strong
I am disabled
I am diabetic.

Eva Murphy (12)
Bottisham Village College, Bottisham

Unlock It

If you want to be the best person you can be
Empowerment is the key
To unlock your true potential
Finding your inner strength, confidence and motivation is
essential
Unlock these things and you will see
How amazing your life can be.

Lily Benton (13)
Bottisham Village College, Bottisham

Peace

I feel peaceful when my brother goes
It is soundless and calming
I feel like I've taken over the chaos
I've caught up to it
Peace
I close my eyes
I fold my arms
I cross my legs
I hear the sound of silence.

Tristan Herridge (12)
Bottisham Village College, Bottisham

Have A Break

Relax, take a break
From social media
Go on a long walk
Savour the moment

Work can be stressful
Don't get mad
Take a deep breath

Remember what made you
Feel happy
Feel carefree.

Tom Hughes (12)
Bottisham Village College, Bottisham

Maybe But You Might...

You might look back at
Your day,
You might think you did
Something wrong,
But you didn't.

You did every night,
You maybe think about
Tomorrow,
And what to do,
Maybe you overthink.

Nataylia Jayne Adams (12)
Bottisham Village College, Bottisham

What You Believe

Everyone has a right to follow what they believe
Doesn't matter who you are or what you are
Just follow what you believe
It doesn't matter what you like or don't like
Just follow what you believe.

Jaiman Bhagat (12)
Bottisham Village College, Bottisham

Being Empowered

Being empowered is
Being confident and strong
Being empowered is
Feeling powerful and in control
Being empowered is
Empowering other people
Being empowered is
Letting nothing stop you.

Daniel Etches (12)
Bottisham Village College, Bottisham

The Deep

What's down there?
The deep, dark depths of the ocean
Any creatures?
I can't see below my feet
The green, murky water lives below me
Oh, I see something!
Help me.

Bella Thomas (12)
Bottisham Village College, Bottisham

Embrace Yourself

Be who you are,
We are all unique,
You should not be embarrassed,
Embrace yourself,
One small thing makes a big difference,
And we are all different,
So live a nice life.

Kleins Tocilla (12)
Bottisham Village College, Bottisham

Football

Football is fun to win games
You can win medals and trophies
FIFA, I've got Akinfenwa
And he's a beast, he doesn't need a team
Ronaldo is the best player in the world.

Alfie Reynolds (11)
Bottisham Village College, Bottisham

Empowerment

Empowerment is key,
Empowerment is dedication,
Empowerment means always working hard,
Empowerment means a breakthrough,
Empowerment is life,
Empowerment is me!

Maya Jaiyeola (13)
Bottisham Village College, Bottisham

Empowerment

Empowerment is when Haaland scores goals
Makes me so happy
I feel like
I am here
With him
Scoring the goals
I can hear the crowd.

Teddy Joy-Staines (12)
Bottisham Village College, Bottisham

Late-Night Phone Call

Pain
It engulfs the mind,
Forces it to wonder,
Grips you till you fall,
That's what a late-night phone call feels like.

Anger
This frustrative measure,
Creating havoc and hurt,
It sucks the hope out of everyone he meets,
That's what a late-night phone call feels like.

Worry
Controls your brain,
It is the joystick and
There is no way to run,
That's what a late-night phone call feels like.

Nervous
A shaky hand holds phone to ear,
Pushes tears to roll down your face,
As you wonder how you got there...

And you picture the person's face.

That's what a late-night phone call feels like.

Jessica Doughty (14)
Higham Lane School Business And Enterprise College, Nuneaton

Expectations

Seriously, being the smart kid is hard
I'm a man of many words, many tricks, many cards
There are plenty of people out there better than me
But I'm recognised for working hard, harder than a bee

Yes, sure, I really love school
The activities, the maths and the large choices pool
Life is simple, I rarely make mistakes
But when I do, my whole class goes insane

"Hey, look at that, I got more than Denis!"
It's such an annoying boast after a test which I didn't fail in
But hey, you must keep calm, life has plenty of choices, what
could go wrong?
A whole lot if you ask me, even if choices aren't strong

With that said, I'm not good at every subject
Like art or PE are the ones I'm most bad in
But I don't let that bother me, life is great!
So I try my best to improve and have possibilities to create

As you can see and wrote, I'm a maths person
My handwriting is bad and my humour is broken
I don't understand what's so hard about numbers?
It's easier than words for sure, vocabulary is large and
trouble

But there is more to me many don't know
I do music, piano and violin, for fun, the otamatone
Though it is such a bother to practise every day
"You have to practise for forty hours" is what some famous
YouTubers always say

Yeah, I don't practise much, my parents get annoyed
But can they just recognise that there are other things I
'destroy'?
Life isn't just music, there are other things as well
I still have a future, I know that as clear as a bell

Back in school, I'm known for other things
A snitch, a goody two shoes, a teacher's pet, the worst
things people think to be
Though I'm a nice guy, people close to me know it
I don't have many though, I am lonely

Sorry, but I am really out of time,
I can't continue, hope you enjoyed these rhymes
People who know me need no explanation
They stereotype me and give high expectations.

Denis Clineanu (13)
Hornchurch High School, Hornchurch

Scripted

It cannot be broken, altered or changed
Trying to do so would drive you insane
Scripted is everything, from happiness to pain
And then it repeats itself all over again
Line by line, the playwright writes
Lines each with an objective in sight
In the script lies a story of hope and light
Not without darkness, however bright
The plan always remains the same
Housed in the shadows, a destructive flame
Empowering, elusive, chaotic, the better the game
Success when all hopes and dreams are slain
Coincidence, or predetermined stakes
"Ridiculous! What nonsense! The script is fake!
I'll do something to prove it's not just fate
Prove it I will!" in denial and irate
The foolish man, his realisation to prove this very script fake,
'Twas purely predetermined fate.

Kahiron Woodruffe (13)
Hornchurch High School, Hornchurch

Again

So... we're doing this again,
Alright, we don't always get things on my first try
Well, at least most of the time,
We always want to be motivated to do things
But we need to do things to be motivated
But getting motivation is hard
Because we try and we fail then we bail
'Cause we don't like negative results
Even if a different party is a fault
But if you, we, just give up
We're giving in to defeat so don't stop trying
Keep on going
Even if you fail again and again and again and yet again
You *can* make change
So you want to give it another try and start all again.

Divine Apinoko (12)
Hornchurch High School, Hornchurch

Gender Questioning

I can be everything sometimes,
I can be nothing sometimes.
I can be a girl sometimes,
I can be a boy sometimes.
I can even be both sometimes.

What I am doesn't apply to you.
What I am isn't your problem.
And if it really matters that much to you
Then I'm proud you care.

If I were a colour, say I was blue,
Would you carry on doing the things that you do?
I highly doubt you'd call me lame
Because in the heart, we're all the same.

Neve Power (11)
Hornchurch High School, Hornchurch

The Boy That Doesn't Know Who He Is

Look in a mirror, what do you see?
A reflection of you and me.
But I know someone who can't see himself
No matter how long he screams for help.

No matter what he does or how he acts
He looks at people who have dreams with envy
Like that kid named Henry.
He does not trust people because people are rude

So this kid is one sad dude.
He had no aspirations in life
So he started to cook with a knife.
He fell in love with cooking and is now a top chef.

Alfie Thorne (13)
Hornchurch High School, Hornchurch

An Update In The System

Two different lives,
Two different rights,
One in the happy white,
Living in the comfortable life, not having to fight.
One in the barn with the animals,
They're being treated like cannibals.
Not allowed to eat, let alone use a fork.
But one man said he had a dream,
That with his plan he could succeed,
So everyone started to believe in the NAACP.
Finally some of the chains set free,
But there was still not total equality.

Kian Davies (13)
Hornchurch High School, Hornchurch

Love The Skin You're In

Love the skin you're in
You're perfect the way you are
Everybody's different but different is a good thing
Love the skin you're in
Don't worry whether you're black or brown
And don't let anyone take you down!

Love the skin you're in
No matter if you're gay or straight
Rich or poor
It doesn't matter what you are
You are you and you are lovely!

April Brett (11)
Hornchurch High School, Hornchurch

Biscuits

Making biscuits was fun but
Zayan's biscuits looked like trash,
Max had the best biscuits
And Teddy's biscuits looked like rocks.

Making biscuits was fun but
Zayan only had five biscuits,
Teddy only had six biscuits
And Max had nine biscuits.

Making biscuits was fun but
Zayan's tasted okay,
Teddy's tasted good
And Max had the best biscuits.

Max Burgess (12)
Hornchurch High School, Hornchurch

Dear 2055

Dear 2055,
I don't think we're gonna survive.
You can even ask Canada about it,
You know forest fires? Well, they've had them.
Any small island will be gone,
All because of the decisions we've made wrong.
You know penguins? Well, they're dying,
All because we are not even trying.
And there is one thing I want to say
And that is
I'm sorry.

Ivan Matidonschi (12)
Hornchurch High School, Hornchurch

Happiness

Happiness is not something you find in a jar
It's not the easiest to try and find
Sometimes it is easy though
If you're depressed or in a bad mental state
The world can make you smile any day
Switch off your phone and go outside
And let nature make you smile
Or it might be a funny TV show
But there will always be something to make you smile.

Freddie Fisher (12)
Hornchurch High School, Hornchurch

Racism

There was a man
Who was Asian
Who ate bran
Then went on vacation

He went to England
Where he was stared at
Because he was Asian
He was treated like a rat

He was Muslim
Just like his friend
He received racial abuse
His feelings weren't easy to mend

Some things change
And some things don't.

Taha Mohammed (13)
Hornchurch High School, Hornchurch

I Can

"You're a girl, you can't play"
"Football's for boys!" they all say
I can play
I can run
Even if I'm a girl
I can play football
I can tackle hard
Girls aren't made of glass
We are strong
So are boys, we are equal
We're not toys

I can play
Any day.

Tegan Harper (12)
Hornchurch High School, Hornchurch

Help

Help!

When people are killed in their own homes
Places they're safe in.

Help! They need but won't get given it.

Help!

People being kidnapped,
Murdered by people who they thought they could trust.
People need help
Then won't get given it when they need it.

Max Cole-Theinmaung (12)
Hornchurch High School, Hornchurch

Why?

Why do we live like this?
Why are the animals dying?
Why can't we have fresh air but instead breathe in pollution?
Why do you litter?
This isn't fair.
Think what you are doing to the world.
We are destroying Earth, which isn't okay.
We need to do better and stop this.

Sarah Mata (12)
Hornchurch High School, Hornchurch

The Life I Enjoy On The Beach

Spring was in the air
The sky blue with care
The flowers blossomed
Bees hummed
Mid-afternoon the sea was blue
Sand dissolved in our hands
Laughing with happiness
Spring was dancing in the air
The sun glowed
All the flowers grew.

Rhsharn Warren (12)

Hornchurch High School, Hornchurch

We Can Play

"Only boys can play"
That's what everyone says
It's not fair
But it's not like they care
Football is my life
This hurts like a knife
I don't care what they say
I'll play every day.

Kyara Alves (12)
Hornchurch High School, Hornchurch

Equality

I wish the world were equal
Who cares if you're
Black, grey, white, Muslim, Christian, heterosexual
It shouldn't matter
You shouldn't treat me differently
I may look different
But I'm not.

Oliver Kersey (12)
Hornchurch High School, Hornchurch

Equal Rights

Equal rights,
Why should we live unequally?
Why do we get different pay between genders?
Why should people of colour worry about being stopped?
Equality matters.
Equality helps everyone,
Equality for all.

Fallon Boxall (12)
Hornchurch High School, Hornchurch

Football

I like football because I am a good goalkeeper
But I can't kick the ball properly
I can save high goals, low goals
Short goals, long goals
I am pretty good.

Mario Oanta (12)
Hornchurch High School, Hornchurch

Our Future World

A world without pollution,
A world where we've found a solution,
Working together,
Creating a perfect world we can be in forever,
A world where teamwork
Has finally made the dream work,
A world without poaching
And instead, we are coaching
Others that we are created equal
And that we must be mutual,
We use solar, wind and sea
And we know friendship is the key,
All together, all as one,
We saved the world and all is done,
And now we can have some fun!

George Khan-Davis (13)
Huish Episcopi Academy, Langport

Beauty Is In Everyone

Beauty is in everyone
It doesn't matter if you're tall or short
It doesn't matter if you're skinny or not
Beauty is in everyone
It comes from within
From being kind and caring
Everyone has beauty
Beauty is in everyone
Even if you haven't unlocked it yet
It's buried deep inside you, I bet
No matter your sex, religion, ethnicity or identity,
We all have some sort of beauty.

Zoë Huntley (13)
Huish Episcopi Academy, Langport

Who Are You?

This time is confusing
Not knowing who you are
But if you keep on believing
You'll get through this burning scar

Not knowing what they think
The spreading rumours and the dirty side looks
But it will end in a blink
And you'll have that life they took

But in the end, it's worth it all
After all that time not able to be you
Go live your life to its full
And go be you.

Elsie Yates (13)
Huish Episcopi Academy, Langport

Midnight Sun

The rain falls as the night goes on
You wouldn't know because your soul is gone
But with your eyes dripping, there is no sun
You think about it but your life is done

Even though we could make it fun
You just need to find the people that can be your sun
Friends, family, they're all there for you
Just speak out and you'll find your way to the people that
are ready for you.

Riley Pope (12)
Huish Episcopi Academy, Langport

I Am Me

We are who we want to be
We don't hold back from our dreams
We can do as much as we put our mind to
I am me

Work hard and don't give up
Enjoy your life while you still can
Let your hair down and embrace yourself
I am me

Love yourself, others and the world
Be grateful for what you have
Learn and achieve everywhere you go
I am me.

Amelia Manning (12)
Huish Episcopi Academy, Langport

Believe

Believe in yourself
Don't let others tell you what's right or wrong
Believe in what's right
Don't let others take you down
Believe in what you like
Don't let others ruin your confidence
Believe in who you are
Show who you really are
Believe
Believe
Believe.

Eleanor Millichip (12)
Huish Episcopi Academy, Langport

Okay

You don't have to shrink to fit in,
You don't have to be like other people,
Yourself is enough.
You have your own mind,
Your own opinion,
Your own voice.
It's okay not to be okay,
Everyone has their ups and downs.

Emily Roberts (13)
Huish Episcopi Academy, Langport

Equality

Growing up you're told to be 'normal',
But you're supposed to be unique.
Most people think that being unique is if you are arty,
But if you have a learning disability you can make a difference,
A bigger difference.

Hannah Berryman (12)
Huish Episcopi Academy, Langport

BLM

Black lives do matter
Remove hatred and see peaceful protests and pro-activity
Black lives do matter
Discuss and talk openly
Break free chains and be set free
Black lives do matter
Time to treat the open wound
We live under one sky, sun and moon
Black lives do matter
Not just one month of the year
Stop shedding crocodile tears
BLM
Educate the world population
End colour oppression.

Aisha Ayor (13)
Manchester Settlement, Openshaw

Revolt - 1381

Blood, fire, tears,
Is it really worth it?
Your cruel, harsh reign
Over the years.

These people,
With nothing, like rats,
Foul, nasty and forgotten.
You think they are useless
Maybe you should think again.

You try to rule with oppression
And deprive them of all they've got,
But now you're playing with fire,
And the dragon has had enough.

These people
Fighting for all they had,
Rising up against you,
Because of one man,
One leader,
One word

Empowerment.

Blood, fire, tears,
Now, was it worth it?

Joseph O'Brien (15)
Ravens Wood School, Bromley

Inspiration By Gaming

Inspiration from above and below,
Many people hope to make it pro,
Games arrive with many chapters and stages,
But my inner demon enrages,
Throughout the series of battles,
Hope is all lost as I jump on the saddles,
I kept on trying to prevail,
But it didn't work as I went down the scale,
Many tragedies along the way occurred,
I kept trying every day and over time I got better,
Giving up now would be totally absurd.

Mert Pastirmacioglu (12)
Ravens Wood School, Bromley

Climate Change

We are powerful; our voices matter
We are a strong community, one that can make a change
We are a community that should be as one
We are the future; our work is not done

She cries and weeps,
Can't you hear?
We're killing her body
But still she gives us her tears

We drink them with haste and greed
But enough is enough
It is us that she needs
Come on, world, we can do this.

Theo Denton (12)
Ravens Wood School, Bromley

Why War?

What is the reason for these damaging wars?
Hundreds of deaths caused by greed,
Countries not obeying the specific laws,
The leaders just carrying on, not listening to any of the many pleas.

Soldiers being brainwashed,
Soldiers being forced,
Young soldiers going into war with their training lost,
Guns and artillery constantly being sourced.

This is real,
This is empowering!

Alfred Mussett (15)
Ravens Wood School, Bromley

Just Remember...

It's all mental,
Be sentimental,
Be your own person,
Play your game,

Don't let a wishbone grow
Where a backbone should be,
Play with passion
Or don't play at all,

Let that tiger free,
To prosper with glee,
Self-sufficiency,
That's all it takes,

Focus,
Focus,
Focus,
There is no magic hocus-pocus.

Seb Shenol (12)
Ravens Wood School, Bromley

Family Trust

When you get down,
And can't get back up,
Ring a friend or one that you trust,
Call them, say s'up.

If a friend doesn't pick up,
And you're out of luck,
Family is there,
And they really care.

To nurse you to health,
Better than you were before,
Smiles on your face,
Love in your core.

Isaac McGonnell (14)
Ravens Wood School, Bromley

We Are Great

No judging
None at all
Nobody is perfect

I'm not perfect
You're not perfect
They're not perfect

But we're great
We all stand out
And that is amazing

Live life to its fullest
No judging
Please, none at all.

Goodluck Adoghe (12)
Ravens Wood School, Bromley

Darkness

Darkness, it came over me,
Like a dark cloud in the sky,
It made me feel cold.

It engulfed me with all its might,
From day into night.

It tortured me with the horrors of my past,
The fears of my present,
And the wonders of my future.

Darkness, it comes in months, days, even seconds to scare
me,
It feels like I am a slave to
the unknown.
Darkness, it happens to us all.

Isabella Edwards (12)
Rendcomb College, Rendcomb

The War Of Ukraine

All you can hear is the sound of pain and fear,
Which makes everyone's thoughts disappear,
Hopes, love and dreams fading away,
Buildings, trees and flowers falling to their end,
Soldiers risking their lives on the battlefield,
Fearing every day, wondering if they will ever see their
family again,
Crashing sounds of bombs and bullets,
Going to sleep, hoping they will see light again,
Saying goodbye to families and children was the worst,
As they never had dreamed of this pain,
No one knows how long it will go on,
This is the war of Ukraine against Russia.

Lacey Stuart (12)
Savio Salesian College, Bootle

Be Proud

Be proud,
Be proud of the voice that you have,
Use it,
Speak up,
Be proud of yourself,
Show it,
Show yourself,
Be proud of the way that you act,
Be yourself,
Do not care what anyone says,
Do what you want to do,
Do not be afraid,
Be what you want to be,
Be proud.

Jack Smith (12)
Savio Salesian College, Bootle

Imagine A World

Imagine a world, a lovely place,
Like a cake, sliced from head to face,
Justice, rights, or so we think,
But we must rise to make a change.
We must imagine such a place
So we can all debate.
Children are the future,
We must treat them this way,
For love, prosperity and to make a change.

Harry Rowlinson (11)
Savio Salesian College, Bootle

Liverpool

The footy match, the footy match,
Salah running down the wing, it's a good thing
Bobby Firmino scoring, I can't stop applauding
Score's up by the second
Hearing all the chants
Seeing all the flags
Big massive flags
I love Liverpool
When I'm walking down Anfield Road.

Charlie Marais (12)
Savio Salesian College, Bootle

Nightmare

The black figure pointed,
The black roses swaying,
The black moon singing,
Like a goodbye forever.
The black figure
Is like a trigger
Pointed towards you,
The black roses screaming,
The black moon gone,
The voice tone,
The dark lone,
Gone.

Marianne Bayliss (11)
Savio Salesian College, Bootle

Family

Family will always be here to bring you lots of cheer
You will always be heard, even when you don't want to say
a word
When they get you a toy you will feel filled with joy
Family will always be everything, always be everything...
Especially to you.

John Harrison (12)
Savio Salesian College, Bootle

People Worry

Worry, a big effect in life
A change in life, a hard change,
"What if I'm not good enough?"
"What if they laugh?"
"What if they leave?"
What if...? What if...?

Morgan Kennedy (11)
Savio Salesian College, Bootle

The Environment

The environment is dying,
We're losing trees, animals and plants!
We need to make a change!
The air is getting as polluted
As the sea is,
How can we stop this?
How can it stop?

Logan Mia Murphy (12)
Savio Salesian College, Bootle